HORSE — 30 MILES (48 KM) PER HOUR

SKATEBOARD — 15 MILES (24 KM) PER HOUR

DOG — 20 MILES (32 KM) PER HOUR

MOTORCYCLE — 120 MILES (193 KM) PER HOUR

NOW THAT'S FAST!: MOTORCYCLES

JACKRABBIT — 45 MILES (72 KM) PER HOUR

HUMAN — 12 MILES (19 KM) PER HOUR

BICYCLE — 15 MILES (24 KM) PER HOUR

NOW THAT'S FAST!
MOTORCYCLES

KATE RIGGS

CREATIVE EDUCATION

Published by Creative Education
P.O. Box 227, Mankato, Minnesota 56002
Creative Education is an imprint of
The Creative Company
www.thecreativecompany.us

Book and cover design by Blue Design
(www.bluedes.com)
Art direction by Rita Marshall
Printed in the United States of America

Photographs by Corbis (Patrick Bennett,
Bettmann), Dreamstime (Gvision,
Sportslibrary), Getty Images (PATRICK
HERTZOG/AFP, Simeone Huber,
FRANCISCO LEONG/AFP, JEFF PACHOUD/
AFP, Piotr Powietrzynski, Quinn Rooney,
Martin Rose/Bongarts, Topical Press
Agency), iStockphoto (Artur Achtelik)

Library of Congress Cataloging-in-
Publication Data
Riggs, Kate.
Motorcycles / by Kate Riggs.
p. cm. — (Now that's fast!)
Includes index.
Summary: A quick-paced, colorful
description of the physical characteristics,
purposes, early history, and high-speed
capabilities of motorcycles—the fastest
two-wheeled vehicles in the world.
ISBN 978-1-58341-914-4
1. Motorcycles—Juvenile literature. I. Title.
II. Series.

TL440.15.R542 2010
629.227'5—dc22
2009002754

First Edition
9 8 7 6 5 4 3 2 1

A motorcycle is a bicycle with an **engine**. The engine helps a motorcycle go fast. Most motorcycles can go 90 miles (145 km) per hour. Some can go almost 150 miles (241 km) per hour!

Motorcycle racers wear special suits and helmets to keep safe

Lots of people ride motorcycles. Some people ride mopeds (*MOH-peds*) in cities. These motorcycles are not very fast. People who like to go fast ride sport bikes. Sport bikes can go on city streets. Sport bikes can race, too.

Some people in big cities like to drive motorcycles instead of cars

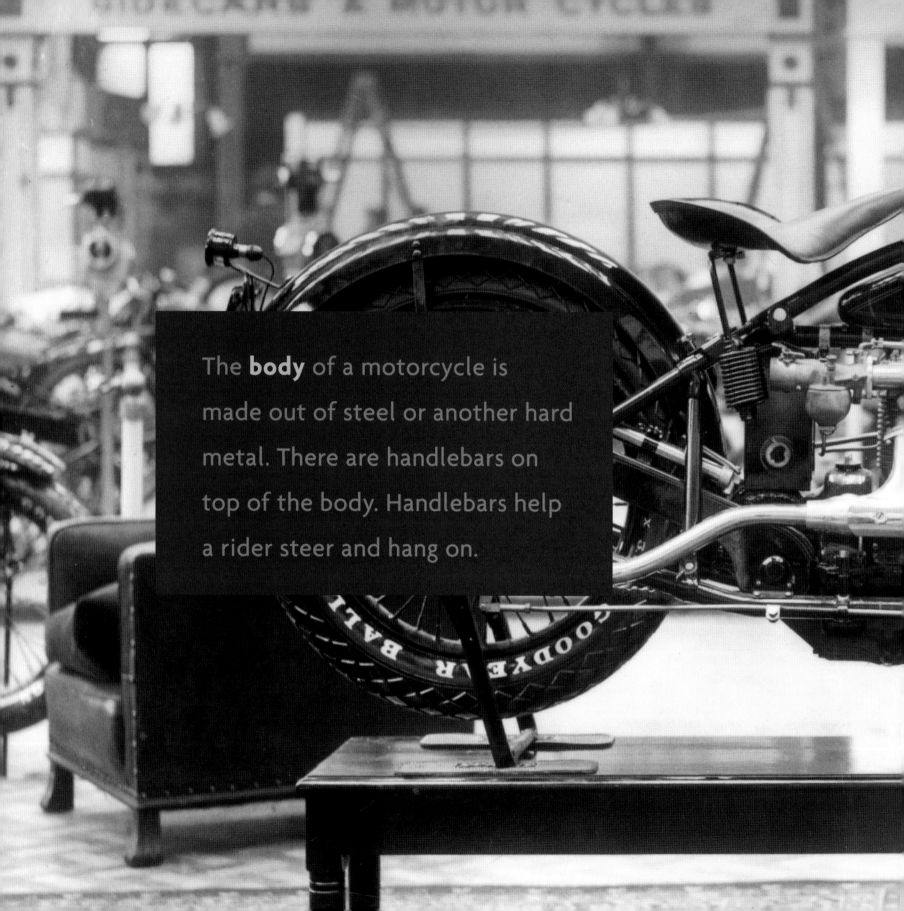

The **body** of a motorcycle is made out of steel or another hard metal. There are handlebars on top of the body. Handlebars help a rider steer and hang on.

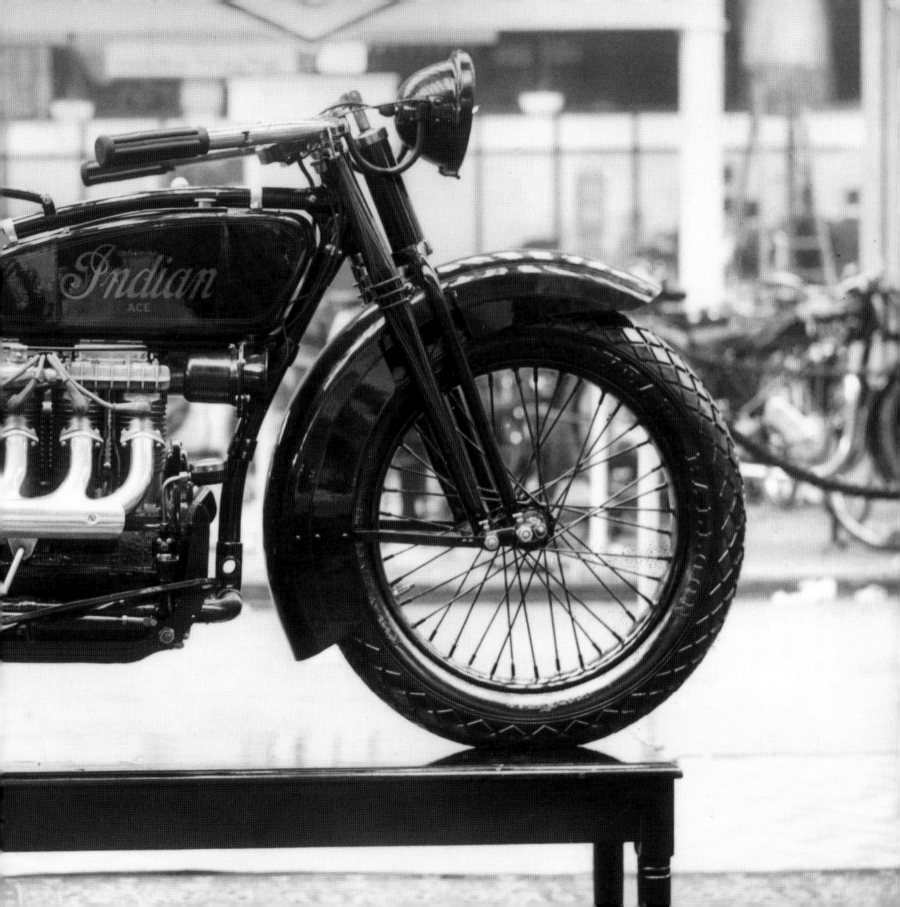

People can drive motorcycles on **paved** roads. They can also drive off the road on dirt paths. The driver controls where the motorcycle goes. He or she wears a helmet for safety. People can fall off motorcycles and get hurt.

Driving motorcycles off the road stirs up a lot of dirt and dust

The first motorcycle was made in Germany in 1885. A man named Gottlieb Daimler (*GOT-leeb DIME-ler*) made it. Later, two men started making motorcycles in America. Their names were William Harley and Arthur Davidson. Lots of people liked Harley-Davidson motorcycles.

Daimler's motorcycle looked very different from those of today

Motorcycle racers grip the handlebars with colorful gloves

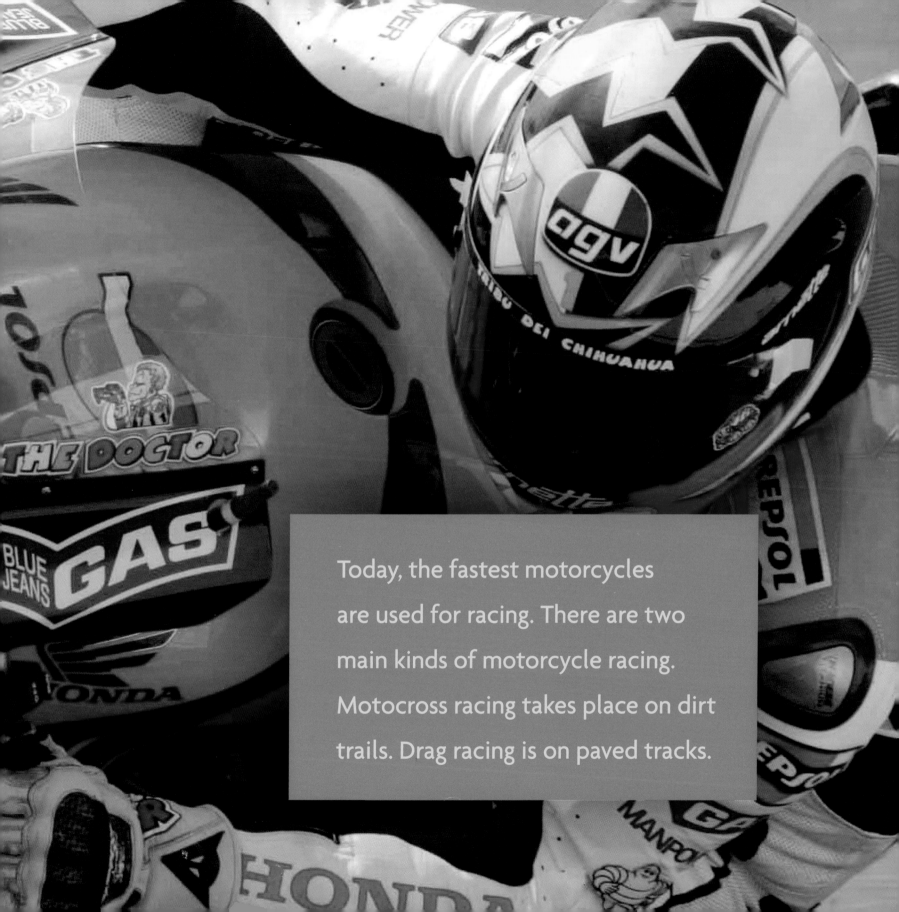

Today, the fastest motorcycles are used for racing. There are two main kinds of motorcycle racing. Motocross racing takes place on dirt trails. Drag racing is on paved tracks.

Motocross bikes can go off the road. People can ride them on sand. They can ride them on mud or rocks, too. Racing bikes are fancy motorcycles. They are light and fast. They are made for racing on tracks.

Motocross racing can be on sand or anything that is not a road

When motorcycles race, they zoom around a track. All of the motorcycles are different colors. But they go so fast that they can be hard to see!

Motorcycle racers have to lean into the tight curves on a track

Many motorcycle drivers like to go fast. They put on a helmet and hang on to the handlebars. They are always ready to take another fun motorcycle ride!

Fast Facts

In 1920, a motorcycle went faster than 100 miles (161 km) per hour for the first time.

The Kawasaki (*kah-wah-SAH-kee*) Z1 was one of the first **modern** sport bikes. It was made in 1971.

Companies in Japan such as Honda, Kawasaki, and Suzuki (*suh-ZOO-kee*) make a lot of fast sport bikes.

The fastest motorcycle in the world went more than 350 miles (563 km) per hour in 2006.

Glossary

body—the main part of something

companies—groups of people who make up a business

engine—a machine inside a vehicle that makes it move

modern—present-day; something that has happened recently

paved—covered with a hard, smooth surface

Read More about It

Goodman, Susan E. *Motorcycles!* New York: Random House Books for Young Readers, 2007.

Hill, Lee Sullivan. *Motorcycles*. Minneapolis: Lerner Publications, 2004.

Web Site

Motorcycle Mania
http://www.kidscom.com/games/motorcycle/motorcycle.html
This site lets you build your own motorcycle.

Index